BLACK COCAINE
AND
COLORLESS BUTTERFLIES

Poetry is the gatekeeper for our souls.

Navah The Buddaphliii

Raleigh, NC

Copyright © 2021 by Navah The Buddaphliii

All rights reserved. No part of this publication may be reproduced, distributed or transmitted in any forms or by any means, without prior written permission.

Rain Publishing
http://rainpublishing.com

Black Cocaine And Colorless Butterflies/Navah The Buddaphliii –1st ed.

IBSN: 978-1-7346106-5-9

Library of Congress Control Number: 2021921878

Dedication

I dedicate my book to the freedom fighters working so hard to bridge the racial wealth gap and abolish systematic racism.

I must acknowledge those on the front lines, facing discrimination, and still having the courage to create a love movement to amplify marginalized voices. You are the true champions of the world leading us towards revolutionary bonding.

I appreciate you.

Thank you!

Introduction

I would like to acknowledge those who inspired me to pick up a pen and create sound, a voice. Prince Rogers Nelson, who truly needs no introduction, was a genius in the eyes of millions. Consider "Purple Rain," what an abstract concept of reality. Let's just look at the title of the band, "The Revolution", What a powerful message. —I wanted to be just like him.

Prince's "Controversy" album cover had the name Joni Mitchell on it. In the late 80's, we did not have Google. I had to know who she was. No one close to me knew. After a few years went by, I came to know she was a white singer, songwriter, and AMAZING. I went and bought all the albums I could find. My favorite album of hers is called "Court in Sparks'. She taught me I didn't have to be a painter to color the world, I could color with my words, vibrant hues, wild, and free. I've always been otherworldly, a bit of a transcendentalist, even as a child. The other children would make fun of me and most of them would call me a witch. Now that I'm all grown up, I see they were right. I am truly magical, especially with a pen in my hand.

Poetry is the process of transformation for the one writing it. As I write, I encourage myself to look at everything in life as a constant change. I've enjoyed the ride on my own brain waves that inspire thought provoking concepts as I fall freely into the universe of imagination. After twenty years as a writer, I finally feel my time and effort is going to pay off. I am stepping out, taking a leap of faith in the title "Black Cocaine and Colorless Butterflies". Please understand, I am not promoting the use of cocaine. I am speaking figuratively about the black struggle I witnessed growing up in a poor, black, crack-cocaine drug infested community. Cocaine did not originate where I lived. The people outside of my community had to bring it there. We all have our demons and our struggles individually and collectively. The community needed a major transformation. I wanted to be a part of the transformation.

I needed to see the drugs removed once and for all. I longed for the community to shed the weight of the black struggles and generational curses that plagued us. I was ready for us to morph into the butterflies we were meant to be as a collective, void of color. Poetry is my offering; it is my contribution to society.

Table of Contents

Crack Cocaine	1
Other Worldly Mind Set	5
A Poem for Prince Rogers Nelson	6
Amber Guyger	7
A Black Mama's Love	8
Black Body Broken Down	9
Commingle	10
Swimming Away from the Light	11
Teach Me and I will Learn	13
She Is Fly Now	14
Razors	15
Band-Aid-Soaked With Tears	16
Prince My Love	17
Windows Down- Inspired by Hannah Brown	18
The Dark Side of Poetry	20
Answers	21
I Want to be What a Man Can Love	22
Sacrilegious Sacrifice	24
A Poem for Two (The Royal Moon)	25
Jonathan Song	26
Build a Shrine for your Dreams	27
Lost in a Train of Thoughts	28
Love, Lies, And Sacrifice	29
Shadow Child	30
Pretty in Stages	31
Three Reasons to Love	32
Whiteness	33

Walking in Paris	34
I Love You to Death	35
My Own Person Jesus	36
Angel's Voice is Broken	37
Do You Dream	38
Phases to the Journey	39
My Skin	42
Real Fortune	43
This is Called Writers Blocked	44
No More Pipe Dreams	46
Noted	48
Call Me Crimson Black and Heroic	49
The Thing That Is Needed	50
A Poet's Song	51
Unheard Of	52
The Planet's Moon	53
No Drug	54
Desiree Deja Vu	55
Life Plays Us	56
Self-Medicating	57
Call This A Rainy Day	58
Fuck The Time I Spent Loving You	59
A Pigeon With A Rose	60
Virus Going Viral	61
Day Moon	62
On the 7th Day	63
Thanks To You	64
White Supremacy Eggshell She Is Walking On!	65

Fading Into My Own "PARADE"	67
Being Tired Of Being Broken	68
Mistakes	69
Once upon a past 1777	70
About Navah The Buddaphliii	73

Crack Cocaine

*I parked my car perfectly
in an available space
across the street,
from the oldest church
in south end of Boston,
to the left of me.
In walks a very attractive male
in his Late 20's
that resembles a century
turning over in its grave.*

*Look like he's been beaten up by life
and his face told the story of his war
and that he was high on drugs.
Drugs that had psychological credibility
which lured him into
the purple state of his mind,
the place where we learn our fears,
a prison for users.*

*Trust me, I know what an addict looks like.
I remember my mom before she died,
but for the life of me, I can't remember
the last time she hugged me.
So, I wondered what he was on
and if he had sniffed coke,
white girl, snowy Caucasus
and all the whistle and bells
of being high.*

*then I got out of my car
and walked towards
him and the way I needed to go.
As I passed, he looked at me
like I was beautiful, and he was mystified.
He said in a voice
made for high definition*

" Well, hey! hey!" and I said hi,
and from what I can see he's no different from me.
We both reside in the dusk of our minds. A
Judas wilderness, a place where I fondle words,
And I find myself.
For him it's a place between the pipe
and his lips. This is where
he loses himself and discovers
the science of angels in
the presence of God
(through a man-made high).
So, I continue to walk down
the street, like I normally do,
reciting poetry out loud.
For about 10 minutes,
give or take, until
I reach the corner of the street
where I worked.

I looked down, and on the ground,
I saw the coolest shadow, it was him.
I looked up and to my surprise,
all I saw was his lackadaisical smile
and eyes that changed like mood rings,
staring directly in my face, and
I can't help but think, could he love
the 9-1-1 eyes staring back at him
(My left-handed personality).

And was he high enough to just
notice the cover
and not care about what it said
inside the book, or maybe
he already read me.
I asked him
are you following me?
And without a moment to
stall he replied
yes, and asked if I was crazy.
His voice sounds like wildly
sung lyrics.
Taken-a-back, I answered to

some, maybe and to others.
A spoken word artist.
And then he asked
me if I wanted to go to breakfast.
Puzzled, judgmental, and full of
Poetry food, I laughed to myself
and wondered who's paying.
See, I grew from a
ghetto garden. I was raised by poverty,
prostitutes, and pimps.
and money was never the root
to all evil, but it was an issue,
an ongoing problem,
and problems make the
worst companions.
So, after the morning
laughter and thank God
not the pill this time.
I snuck in a question
and asked him was he high?
And what was he on
acid, ecstasy? I know it
wasn't weed because I did that.
He said it was hard.
I said what is hard.
He said cocaine, I said crack.
Yeah, crack, a stone fragment
those in the trap call crack
rocks and away out.
I pause, then he says
"Come on let's go get breakfast"
I explained to him
how life isn't a race
It's a chase and we all
got dreams to catch.
And how I would love to,
but I've got this thing I can't
shake and sometimes it gets
in the way, it's called a job.
Now between him being high
and me being INSANE
I mean,

A POET.
I thought
him and I would make either
the perfect match
or a recipe for disaster.
So, here is where
Jesus finally took the wheel.
And our conversation
ended in a breadbasket at this
cute cafe, we are having breakfast at Tiffany's.

Other Worldly Mind Set

My mind is a finely tuned library
You have to be steady when
You study inside this unbraided universe

You have to wear a daredevil's smile and have
A gun smoke charm about you to show the other
Worldly explorers that bravery can also look reckless

When you enter this groundbreaking galaxy
Adorned with a neon rainbow and peacock feathers
You must remove your crown
Show us the blood

Stains on your soul and expose the
Monosyllabic queen gated inside you
Show us your red flag and how it works

Did you teach it how to escape the avalanche
That shadows it travelers like you don't come with
Warning signs just guessing games

And my guess is you are probably going
To play all the mind games you can
Am I right

A Poem for Prince Rogers Nelson

I believe it was the sawdust of summer when I found your voice in a shadow of a song. It reminded me of my past hurt. You sang so beautifully of lilacs and photogenic water, you built harmonies powerful enough to save angels in a storm.

*Quickly I caught on and held tight to your butterflies you called lyrics. You spoke of love like you had a **doctrine** in it. I thought, for men, love was a learning curve. You proved me wrong. You did not just create music and magic; you birth colors out of sound and called them stories.*

You blurred the lines between reality and fantasy. I bet your music is similar to the way God speaks. I bet you discovered a guitar inside of a black deity and the piano inside of a white devil's broken heart.

*Prince, I bet you can play anything, even the fossils of flowers.
Your music is an endless drug, a purple high. Listening to you made me feel like all four seasons cuddled up with a kiss.
Tell me, when did you get tired of playing love songs?*

When did balancing the moon and a microphone become all too much for you? Who choked the life out of your vocal cords? Damn! I would give almost anything to hear you live again! I wear your songs in my ears like heirlooms. Oh Wait, I think I get it. Is this how you go beyond means of self to teach us dead silence is music too?

Amber Guyger

News announced today "cop kills a man in his own home."
Mistakes his apartment for hers, mistakes him for a burglar or
an easy target!

My Granny says, "I bet she is a white woman and he was a black man."
She used the word "was" since Botham is dead. Granny says
"Cops killing black bodies has been normalized since forever."

Three days later the news released her name and photo.
My Granny was right. She is a white woman with
Klansman's robes for eyes looking to kill a black man.

Amber, tell me did you sit in your car for 15 hours carving
Botham's name on the bullet that killed him before
going to his apartment?

Did you want his apartment to reflect the same color as
the red mat in front of his door?
Oh, you didn't notice that.

Did you just decide to take a shot in the dark,
while Botham was in his home resting effortlessly?
It was too dark for you to see that was
not your apartment but lit enough to see him to shoot him in his chest.

Amber, I bet your heart is cut from the same
cloth as your mother's "All Lives Matter" Tee Shirt.
Oh, you thought we didn't see that.
Botham's mother says his heart was made by angels.

A Black Mama's Love

A black mama's love comes with a pen filled with amiable love.
A pen ready to write her progeny well and safe.
The first line reads:
"I played peek-a-boo with you just
to brand a smile across your face."

A black mama hides for a moment
then shows you her hands
and the happiness that fell in the rain today.
She tells you of her memories
Of her counting all ten fingers and toes
then grinning and thanking God.
She hopes one day you will feel joy and moonlight all around you.

A black mama ain't always perfect
and her approach for shielding you from harm's way
can sound a lot like cloudy rocking roads,
with too many folks in them.
She wants your path cleared enough for incalculable possibilities.

She wants you to be able to love safe enough to sway to the rhythm
of your own beat and be watchful of the grey areas to come.
Mama, tells you the dangers about expressing puppy love
When it comes to black boy's growing bones.

Black boys can't be tamed in a white world. They do not come
endowed with leashes, so they do not sit and stay. Their egos have no
home training, but cops do. They are trained to end black triumph
unapologetically with no remorse or accountability.

Mama makes you a cake and pretends it is your birthday.
She tells you, "make a wish and blow out the candles."
She wants to celebrate you while she still can, and you can still smile.
She wants to write more lines about you, but her pen ran out of ink.

Black Body Broken Down

My black body unhinged at the seams
half of me laid out over concrete puddles
My Achilles heel set out on an adventure, which can
lead to my permanent downfall.

My shoes are gold mines in retrograde, trying
to walk to the rhythm of an out of tune heartbeat
Most black bodies are newborn poems, they need a strong
foundation and constant work, so the writer can have a leg to stand on.

Commingle

Disrobe the rhythm in my heart.
Let it ceremonialize its own unsympathetic departure
in the dead of winter.

Let it yowl like a pack of coyotes.
Then let the wind take the
melody to Jupiter in Capricorn.

Swimming Away from the Light

*I looked far beneath the surface
of your face, I found pain and blood boiling
like an ocean
that can't swim away.*

*I found beaten bones
and so many unholy wars of
yesterday.*

*Tell me, have you seen your reflection lately?
Did you see us ALL,
honey and purple wildflowers?*

*Hiding behind the only halo
we hallucinated and worn in other's memories who denounced us.*

*Remember how we
wrapped them so carefully
in paper-ma-shay pearls and perception.*

*We found how effortlessly
it is to play hardball
with imagination.*

*I wish our worlds didn't
fall apart and break so easily!
I wish purgatory wasn't
attached to our gravestones
that reads, "Here lay the
two olive branches never extended."*

*I wish we weren't left to die.
If only they knew sage and a hug was our cure.
Then we could have done
the shadow work only
performed by God.*

*Now we will never know how
the Elohist befriend*

it's demons and not kill them.
Maybe in some strange way they
know this is the only thing keeping them alive.
I wish tomorrow wasn't already dead,
like fresh cut roses
with buds of innocence.
Death knows so well
how to mirror life.

It placed warning signs on pedestals
high enough so that all may see, but what I see is
we are a journey and not on one.

We are a continuum of blurred lines
drawn in sand and sky.
Dying wasn't the problem
and living was never the answer.
I never asked to be delivered from evil,
I just wanted to know, why
was it created?

Teach Me and I will Learn

*What I have mastered is the art of love and the
understanding that some hearts are worth fighting for
and some are not.*

*See here, the scar's love left, when it LEFT.
See how remorse has its limitations
when it came to you loving me?*

*I still see the imagery when I think hard enough
how I once smiled
like a full-grown sunflower under moonlight.*

*I also see how your love vandalized what I feel for you.
How I trusted you, not knowing my
faith would need an accountability partner.*

*Now your eyes sickened and contrite, ruled by
Venus and lust, which caused my
tears to look like diamonds in the rough.*

*If only tears could talk instead of just fall.
They would probably tell us what love sounds
like underwater.*

*This pain isn't poetic it is just words
massaging deeper wounds.
My heart is a powerful stanza, standing all alone.*

She Is Fly Now

She plunged to the lowest level
of the ocean and grabbed
a handful of Mermaid's dung.
She flew back up and
smeared it across the sky.

Holy, bloody, butterfly wings
Batman! What happened to her
standoffish mind, or her cry for
help? Who accidentally slipped a
roofie into her heart.
She's flying!
She's flying!
She's gone!

Razors

*Razors, did you know, they show a kind act of love?
Picture me, 18, not taking life or myself seriously enough.
Well not as seriously as some would take razors and love.
See, I discovered one day, just horsing around on a carousel ride
of trauma, we can all chase dreams, but few of us will catch them.
I discovered, I needed to be careful where I was dreaming to.*

*Careful, like I was in love. Careful like I was using razors to chisel through
the ground until I reached the earth's bones. I also discovered, rubbing razors,
and love the wrong way can feel as if you had a brush with death.
See, God got it wrong. Love should be barricaded by stonewalls instead of hearts and songs.
Love is messy and poetic, and it carries a ratchet razor that I often use.*

*Understand, cuts are messengers too. They tattletale and dry snitch every
chance they get about my anger, my fear, and my secret stash of razors
to a world that couldn't possibly understand. What the hell? Didn't they
get the memo? My pain is shy, and I don't know how to love "normal,"
just insane, and misunderstood. The truth is, I am looking for someone to
feed on, and stay full-off-of, and understand. Until then, I stay quiet, barely hear.*

*I got a voice as loud as silence and in the bedroom, I make as much noise
as a butterfly. Ironically, they call me Navah the Butterfly because when I speak
It's poetic with no safe words; just someone else's slit wrist pouring out of me.
O Negative, premeditated blood drops, leading down a trail to what is really wrong
with me. I confess, I am sick and creative. I am something you can't just
simply sleep off. Sweet dreams. It is going to take more than razor sharp
words and music that sings to what's between my legs to fix me. It's going to take GOD,
running from every direction at once just to come and hold me.*

*I will tell them, "I don't know how to stop using razors, or a world around me as a mirror."
A world that is someone else's Heaven and someone else's Hell. Sometimes, I play the hero and
the villain too, as I try to pick up the pieces of myself (five at a time), to put me back together
again.*

*I CAN'T! So, I hurt with razors for now, but one day I will hurt with kindness, and I will be
amazing! And I will teach me how NOT to use razors, and how NOT to lead love down a
dark alley where blood
don't wash away so easily.*

Band-Aid-Soaked With Tears

When your happiness is attached to a
sunset playground be careful,
try not to get sunburned.
There are no boundaries set
or ground rules on this uneven playing field
just hungover sunflowers, a premature downfall that once stood
tall in the razor blade, green grass.
Disguised as rose petals, look closely
and try not to step on the caterpillars.
Someday they will be butterflies.
With that being said, understand
what you are and what you are meant
to survive are two different things.
I have always admired the way
you referred to yourself in
the 3rd person. Why did you stop?
What part of your heart came unhinged
at the dreams?
Who silenced you?
Didn't they know you can't
close these type of doors
once they're open?
You can't just unsee what is there.
You can't just swim away from these many tears, and there
are not enough band-aids to cover them

Prince My Love

These feet in these shoes
Are landmines in retrograde
Trying to get to you
My Achilles heel is scared to
Adventure off into some paisley
Hallucination or the unknown
For you
I just want to place
Purple wildflowers
All around lake Minnetonka
For you
But there is a crack
In my halo and I can't fly
That far or fast anymore
I still have my dreams though
And the vivid one the night after
You passed
Orange always looks good on you
And by the way I cried so much
Over you until my tears looked
Like diamonds in the rough
I can write you for days
I can deeply massage words
That will penetrate through
The toughest Souls
Where was your
Accountability partner that day
Perhaps Venus or in some old
Room standing next to an elephant
But Prince I know now you are being
Cared for by butterflies
And pleased by a million pleasures
So Til then my love.

Windows Down- Inspired by Hannah Brown

*Windows down
and I insist on whispering through the windowpane.
Words that talk to pillows.
Words that leave lips smothered in honey,
lips frozen on cheeks and forehead. I can only feel them now and salted covered fantasies.
I want to know what made you,
because I can still feel your winter-fresh permanent kisses you left on me
and see what reminds me of your lips 18 feet outside this hard to open window. And since I
can't open it, I place this right-hand front palm on glass.
Staring into a memory of what I may never have again. And I breathe in deep,
Hurting my lungs with air, a cigarette and a loneliness too hard to swallow or let go.
I no longer feel beautiful. Why did you leave me trapped between words
and a window I struggle to open.
A window that has no smile to share
or clean glass to look through.
I know, windows don't share smiles, but people do, that look closely in them.
And I imagine I see their smiles through the heavy black eyelashes and hard to lift eyelids from
crying, see them through the wetness of my eyes and the window where I watch my own soul's
departure.
And these tears I cry does nothing for you or me, or this romantic sadness you left by this
window with its arms wrapped around me. I want to lift this window and scream to you
"COME BACK!"
I can't breath. And did you know
right before you left, I wanted to ask you
"Couldn't you find another word for goodbye,"
That sound more like art and
Are you sad?
Are you sorry?
Or are you both?
That you left sorrow woven between our hearts.
I want to lift this window and ask the wind to carry it and the thought of you away,
But this window is hard to open.
And my left hand is busy writing vivid poems about you.
And as I write, I am torn apart by words and the remaining
Punch line I did not get a chance to throw at you. And by the way, did you know
Because of you, I sing tearful lullabies in the key of blues while nearby noble neighbors shut
their windows. I know they much rather hear Jaw-dropping voices singing in the key of
evergreen. Sung in made-up words
Like flute-ty and crystal-ly*

But instead, they hear me.
I sound like rain beating against cardboard boxes taped to windows.
I wish my voice was lightly rung wedding bells.
I wish my name was Bell.
Then I would seem just as angelic as clouds and earth flowers, Just beautiful enough for you to love me. I wish you had to love me. I wish promises weren't made to be broken.
Promises that speak lies through rose-colored tint windows and under your bashful breath mixed in with Delgado lines. Meaning lines can hold truth as thin as a whisper, and the silhouette of your whisper, will forever run circles around my mind, with the scent of you lingering I will forever smell the lavender teardrops that fell from my eyes into your mind.
A mind quieter than a closed window.
And slightly noisier than moving butterfly wings. I can hear you saying
"Navah open up the window."

The Dark Side of Poetry

The ocean, it's just a wetter version of the sky, a 'graveyard' of poetry that broke into my heart, and opened my eyes, and I saw the brightest darkness mirror reading handwritten dreams cuffing the stars consoling the rain who tears laughed, and in that laughter, I heard the words "God hates you."

These insulting tears that only once God could hear now speaks to me with warring tongues. And I had nothing deep to say, just a crushed sentence, a pile of regret, a sky that jumped on my train thought and we went from an angelic- blue to a halo of black. God, I do apologize if you feel like I have displeased you.

You see I have been searching for a weightless god because the others are too heavy and too weak like watered-down gospel, weak like the dark side of poetry. Weak like a religious inside joke no one gets. Forgive me for you know everything. I don't so, tell me, am I a self-portrait of you? Will you promise to clean dirty lost souls like mine?

Will u forgive me for having an enchanted mind? You see, I often mistook you for a poem that has never been written. Mistook you for masculine words that became undone.

I mistook you for a selfless father that has more than one son, mistook you for a sky filled with multiple sunsets. I know nothing of you. You unseen god. Tell me, am I of the other god? am I his fleshly creation standing outside of my normal heartbeat and on the footnotes of his story. Standing, breathing whirlwinds of soundless music into the lungs of his bible. The lungs of his heaven that often resembles the bloodstains in his hell; blood that flows throughout my veins, and into an anthem of sorrow, sung with broken tongues; sorrow buried in all kind of ancient languages.

And I sit in this hell crying with roses that's been wounded by his thoughts and his words shoved into each other, and I hate this so much that I stripped down to pain, and I am exposed, naked with caution, and I can see that my heart is a jealous god; also an egotistic ghost filled with love I never felt. A love that has no title. A love I am not entitled to feel and why should I be.

When that god knows I am a sleepwalking addict high off of pain. Why should I be when he sees I am as useless as a headless butterfly. When I should be more like the ocean, just a wetter version of the sky.

Answers

*Stillness was so quiet when I spoke fidelity,
but I heard baritone singing of angels. Deep thoughts of spiritually
will be the most high power manifested in me,
to interpreted who are the 12 tribes of Israeli
America's seed scatter among hypocrisy.
And nations of deceit bring turmoil to brainwash me.
Beat me and defeat me, but the most high has shielded me from North America's confusion.
Promising beneficial dreams that are just an illusion, of something fundamental knocking at my door.
Telling me it's Jesus and why don't answer.
No, why don't you wake up to the fact that there
Is no heaven above and no hell below.
It's the image in front of you that's the likeness to behold! When the first and the last time
you saw a spirit in the sky and if you
did, you was misleading yourself. I believe it was the clouds going by.
Holy Mary mother of god! They got you believing in miracles they have not seen.
Mathematical thoughts planet in your soap, food, water, churches even
your thoughts when you sleep. And you will find yourself looking for answers, but where are all your answers buried? With your ancestors.*

I Want to be What a Man Can Love

Man is on the outside of what he believes he is in
Man is an earth dancer that knows not his mind, body, and spirit
For when he knows himself his knowledge becomes cruelty
He is then overtaken by the moment he finds truth
and at that time he forgets everything he has learned
and identify himself as being exhausted by life
and what he thinks could be love
He is aware, life is a surprise and death can't be less than one
But unaware he is a child of chance, two sides of one coin, daring and original; he is dangerously
beautiful and ugly at the same time
It is like he is blessed and cursed with a cross heart that is not ready to be happy and a mind
craze like those that talk about heaven and
don't have a hell to compare it to
It is because man's world is an empty dream,
surrounded by chaotic love, a love best kept at a distance
Further than the moon and the sun detached from space breaking earth, and it is here where
man is able to reach back in time
And inhabit a human experience over and over again
This godless custom he has grown accustomed too
And for what? Well he wants to feel if he can truly love
And remember what he loves
Not the kind of Sebastian crystal gem
embroidered lies, these unwanted kisses
Lies that smile with such belief love
No, not that kind and not the love that comes
with small sensual sacrilegious screams
No, I am talking about a love that is more than just felt
a love other than just a mirage of echoes
A love that would not be unremembered
and gently carried by sands of time
A love that will run forever
like tears that will never dry
A love that will allow its pain to get its point across
by telling all about how it is to live with its own death
and heal what it has yet to be certain of
I want to see man fondness for pain turn into power
inside of a cocoon and become the influential butterfly
I believe he has been all along
A kind of man that will no longer be afraid to give mary J. Blige that real love

Someday I want to be like that
Someday I want to be more than just noise
More than just unwanted breath
I want to be what a man can love

Sacrilegious Sacrifice

Wounded air I breathe in as I think of you
Crystal sand beneath my feet and still I struggle to walk towards you
Candy blue sky I see settling inside of you no room left for me
so I cry without you.
Pleasurable pain roped around my throat
and my mind is high from the thought of you I smoked.
I open a memory full of suitcases
where you hide your misery and your many faces
I AM YOUR SACRILEGIOUS SACRIFICE you needed for just a short time
I know now loving you is harmful to my mind and damn near a crime.
You sing yourself out of rainbows time and time and again
Unsettle soul I will love you until my world is over and yours begin.
Please tell me you will give my love for you a fighting chance to win
Trust me on this I know our bond was never made just to be broken
I AM YOUR SACRILEGIOUS SACRIFICE you needed for just a short time
I know now loving you can be harmful to my mind and damn near a crime.
I disassembled the universe just to find you
dismantled the earth just to get inside you
In the dark I hid the stars just so I can find you
discovered god just to remind you.
I can't and will not live a life without you
I AM YOUR SACRILEGIOUS SACRIFICE you needed for just a short time
I know now loving you can be harmful to my mind and damn near a crime.

A Poem for Two (The Royal Moon)

*The above blameless clouds and a sluggish silvery skyline
are an ivory pearl ruling like royalty in an unforgiving sky.*

*In it are innocent stars accused of passionate crimes
that are bridged together like a crucifix overlaying the night.*

*The once-powerful now defenseless lights are mourning their very own
glow that fades away like compliments. They are fully vulnerable as sitting ducks*

*Waiting in the welkin. These heavenly-bodied creatures
confined to grey areas and hummingbird grey lines are*

*Judged by a non-maternal heaven. When did the sky become similar to a prison, a jailhouse
without bars, the slammer for stars? My guess is It started with the*

*Imbalanced moon's tall tale of what could have been. Her words traveled
faster than a Halley's Comet going to and from every planet leaving bits and pieces of itself.
Just imagine being that high from being high, and still, her highness falls for the stars. Those
sparkly poetic gems, beautiful Asian flowers,*

*Orchids of the night. Only they are alluring enough to sweep the moon
off her feet while the rest of the milkyway collapses at it.*

*It is unfair these upright things that bless the twilight are birthed in a moment they can't
outrun, and still, they bolt through a sightless journey as they are chased*

*By a galaxy of everything from satellites to black holes, but mostly what the scorned moon feels.
If only they were shooting stars quick enough to escape from the*

*Crescent moon's mood swings and her Luna Eclipse of roller coaster rides. So ludicrous you
swear it was a dream or maybe some sort of nightmare.*

*Perhaps the celestial moon was never taught that love is not a stranger to some but to most and
that stars are not gods, but poets. And each night they spit a fine-tune*

*Poem to the retro sky about how unsafe space feels in the dark and how there are no good nights
there. Just empty goodbyes and as for the Royal Moon she got exactly what she wanted, and it is
for the precious stars to feel just as damaged as she is.*

Jonathan Song

I let him know how I smiled at the way his hand fitted inside of mine, and oh how I fancy his love, but instead of love all he handed me; whatever he found lying around, and an unwanted bye.

I let him know I love him with no gray areas attached. If you know him, then you know he has a heart that is hard to catch. shielded by a rain forest of mirrors glazed over in metallic black.

Still, in my darkest hour, I mustered up holocausts of hope, as I watched my love and what he called love walk away on a free-falling tightrope. I could hear his words faintly in the distance over and over again.

"In time what will be will be."
"In time what will be will be."
"In time what will be will be."

His words felt less like a song and more like our eulogy, but I am still hopeful and will love him until my heart is worn out. I will not let my mouth forbid me to speak what my heart needs him to hear.

What do you do with a heart that won't give up or let go, what has let go of it? But I am still hopeful like twins in a crowded womb, hopeful like waiting for a chance.

And one day I will teach my soul to give sunlight back to the sun and continue to hold the dear words Jonathan never sang.

Build a Shrine for your Dreams

*Open up yourself entirely. Let your dreams shape a new you,
let them give you the perfect skin, rosemary thoughts, youthful words and a dusty rose colored
lace bow to set off your coffee-stained smile.*

*There are no unwanted dreams here to beat your soul with,
only the wet ones swimming inside of you, chasing after storms to stay full off of. Tell me, have
you ever been hugged by a dream?
Dreams have arms wide enough to fit around the sun.*

*See, when the earth goes mad you must build a shrine for your dreams, and let it not make
sense, play with its magic, and let it show you the things you never imagined, like the sun
swimming inside of a rose.*

*Dreams are a drug we can't put down, a wonderful habit, an art form of bigger things to help
us come. Dreams wait for you every night in a bed of too many I love you's. See our minds are a
gateway to heaven and dreams are the Angels that protect it.*

Lost in a Train of Thoughts

*Your voice sounds like future music,
something that has not been thought up yet.
I can only imagine dreamlike tones,
it's true entertainment for the mind.*

*And I dreamt up your voice walking slowly for miles in my thoughts.
I picture your voice to be a symphony
of morning glory vines and violins*

*Stringing me along, and this private
concert is for my ears only, and I am playing
musical chairs on a runaway train of thoughts.
I tell you how words don't always need sound.*

*They find ways to cut corners and
I found a way to find you and you
stay uncut, well kept in a well Lit
corner of my thoughts.*

*Your voice is a lighthouse, it is
luminescent when I am cocooned
in a dark corner standing on a
colorless ground fearing the butterflies
that cloud my Judgment
and make me
lose my train of thought.*

*Your strength teach me to sleep
peacefully with fire in my heart,
and smoke in my eyes. You feel to me like
Tuesday in an Indian summer, and
healing thoughts.
In you, I found a safe house,
sweet nothings, and holiness in your blood.
When we speak in person
we will only speak in smiles,
and yours always reminds
me of an angel protecting my thoughts.*

Love, Lies, And Sacrifice

Will I lie of love?
To the one
Who is as true as day
How shall I deny his smile?
In light of earth's morning
These questions have burden my blood and choked my breath
As I lie of a million pleasures
Pretending he has pleased
Knowing still not one he shall fulfill
Curse not my lying lips
for they are a hero to his heart
I will abandon my joy
to protect the soft part of his heart
I will show him not my saddened self
but piercing arrows of strength
though I long to hide
in the shadow of weeping willow trees
Instead I ask myself
How can I cause pain to the one
whose heart for me is a glow?
In me love is frail
And my words
Are longing to lie
And the truth is
In love I am not
Still I allow him to consume me
And I shall obey our togetherness
for it is wise
Unlike his foolish heart
too far gone in love to see
I pretend to grieve not
I bid my happiness farewell
And sacrifice for him when others dare not

Shadow Child

Camouflaged in the womb
nickname invisible sightings
That no one sees.

Undetectable smiles
young premonition
A hidden prediction
waiting to be born.

You are shared
blood and bone
still marinating in
an immature vision.

Pretty in Stages

*I am somewhere lost
in a hostile dream
and the South End.*

*There are no more feathers
on my skin and stars in my eyes.
It is the second week of a gothic
autumn and winter is waiting its turn.*

*I am swinging
on a golden sunset
enjoying someone else's fun.*

*When you are this pretty
you don't just delete your social media,
You delete your entire social life.*

*This is a great way to rest
peacefully in Life.
My mind is the beautiful scenery I live in.*

Three Reasons to Love

I don't want to count.
Please don't make me.
I want to mate like a love bird
On the first day of spring.

I want to give wings to my high spirited passion
and fly to unknown whereabouts in you that no
one has ever reached before.

I can stare at you and never get tired
You are so exciting to look at with your
Purple velvet lips and locus eyes that shimmer.

Your body looks perfect like someone
oil painted you.
Now if I could just get you tattooed
on my eyelids.
It will go so well
With the picture of you
hung on the wall in my mind.

You are the star on every stage you stand.

My human heart
only beats for you.
So I am going to need you
To live always.

Whiteness

*The problem with
whiteness is, it is
empty, incomplete
and does not know how*

*to operate when it
removes the hate
and the toxicity
it has comfortably*

*grown accustomed to.
It goes back to an
infant state of being
and unfortunately*

*can't think for itself.
It is Vulnerable
anyone can come
in and infiltrate*

*with hidden agendas
and manipulation.
White folks learning to
unpack your whiteness*

*lacks spiritually and
will take you a lifetime
to do. A lifetime you don't have.*

*Whiteness is
a conundrum rooted
in slave blood and
capitalism. Whiteness
has no duality.*

Walking in Paris

*I heard Paris is a city for walking and I say so is
everywhere else. I see the brighter side of things.
I see crystals, stones, made to heal and restore souls
Do you need restoring?*

*I need my Partner's laugher and the abundance of love
They give. I need their face, that reminds me of the
opening of every beautiful Prince song. I need a state of bliss since
I outgrew the space that no longer served a purpose in my life.*

*I don't need Paris to represent my love or desires. This power is all mine.
I am strong will and soft to touch, warm and polished for days.
I groom greatness.
I have hugs of hope for all those I love,
I truly believe a bruise soul can still smile.
I gave life to all that are willing to paint themselves beautiful.
And I will continue to paint myself
with frost-blue colored wings
on a fly ass canvas of me walking in Paris.*

I Love You to Death

My heart a wounded soldier set out for battle with gaping wounds
painfully fresh from baring crosses in chris like gardens
I fight a fight and I always win. I battle on this
field, made for God's virgins and doves that continuously cry.
In this holy city I play God and I carry with me a Love full of mistakes.
I bear no tears yet armed in them. Age tears from past lovers
who could not get the best of me, they're all dead now and buried with no apologies. See, it is
love that turns hero into villain. So, I'm ready, ready for battle, ready for protege called God's
weapons.

I am prepared to drag them through hell with me. They are the same as me. We were both born
in the year of the light. We are the Fallen ones, falling hard like hearts do when in love and our
hearts smudged with the blackest residue. And when face to face our graveyard of a soul looks
uncomfortable.

Our skin indigo rose petals surrounded by Romeo and Juliet's death. We are an old idea of
love. We learn in our dreams since childhood. The funny thing about love is it doesn't need a
reason to be or not to be that was never the question.

So, here we fight in breathtaking details together we are war. No love will be made here.
Just skull crashing hymns with violent words of painful poetry. Here words hurt.
Together we speak a glass language, take shots, and get drunk off of one another's blood leaving
our lips armed and dangerous, laced with the purest poison.

We kiss with thrown fist. We have little to no power over our own cobblestone heartbeat that
beats no louder than the sound of invisible noise beating on compromised ear drums.

And if you listen closely, each beat is a battle cry. So, this battle cries moonlit tears buried in
love songs and our tears repeatedly rip through ink tearing into each others souls with sharp edge
fossils of "I love you" and "I love you" feel more like bullets
piercing through High School sweethearts and Newlyweds.

We fall to our death, though some mistook it for falling in love.
The same love that taught us
Poems tell stories. Tall tales of what could have been. And we die with this love and melt away
like broken candles in a galaxy that shined like diamonds a thousand skies high. We lived a
new end because we loved like suicide. So it is only fitting for our headstones to read love is
nothing less than exciting and can only be measured by impact.

My Own Person Jesus

*I watch the sky take
notes from the stars
I saw how they are
loyal by blood.*

*It was beautiful to see
I made a mental note
Of it and it left the right side
of my brain with paper cuts.*

*I will heal as I always do
Besides, pain is a place
we all go to visit and not stay.*

*I do all the things that are
required of me
when I love someone
I make it my
goal to make sure they are
more beautiful than how
I found them.*

*I won't just paint
them a rainbow on a white
soft bone canvas
and walk away
with footsteps just
echoing along
I will become a part of them
and embrace their most holiest of ghost.*

*Take pleasure in pleasing their body
like they were my own personal Jesus
and I am nailed to their landscape of open arms.*

Angel's Voice is Broken

Stable, warm, posy water
On the other side of my window
I want to feel its comfort
I want to fill up its space.

Instead of the empty room
Where I sit marveling at a
Cocaine, black, and shadow
worked white photograph of you.

My angel, I am missing you
Your voice is broken and I can't hear
You anymore. Blue rose petals are
Falling I can't see you anymore
I tell my soul to not search for you anymore.

If this heart-rending picture of you can speak
I imagine it would mouth the words your
blithering hair held the scent of late October's rain
You were always autumn asking to be loved
I still hear your pain.

And did you know
Sandra's garden appears in your photograph
with dreamscapes of white lilies dancing in a
Labyrinth with falling leaves far and near
I wish I was there.

Do You Dream

Do you dream? Is it jarring?
Is there a palpitating truth I can find even
If it is delicate like a cat's curiosity?
I just want to see it come with the sun and
without its lavishing rays in the way
I want you to dream me to move fast,
be bountiful, and not overlooked
when I make mountains scream.

Dream me to be the extravagant water-
Sign-cancer so I can flow freely to be my
counterpoise self.
Allow me to turn over
a new leaf while using your heart as a stepping
Stool to get inside your mind to become your every fantasy.

As you dream I will change the structure of time.
Swim in your careful touches and get lost in your
garments. I am trying to reach your mind like undelivered
love letters. I want to explore more than your dream.
I will only taste the part of you that melts away.

Phases to the Journey

*One day I was confidently walking
taking notice to the wind carry
all the caution it could
I tripped over a dirt bank
and fell into a massive holt*

*The owner was not there
Just lumps of its fur
I wonder if the animal was
cold or maybe it did forest drugs
to stay warm*

*I thought about how once
I saw a squirrel sniffing
something that looked like powdery
black cocaine
I admired its freedom
no policing or protesting just nature
doing its will*

*I climb up out of the hole and
Began to walk again
My is journey is forever
changing and the challenges
That comes with it hold wisdom to get me
Through the next phase of life*

*I fall and
And get back up in due time
A lesson learned
Is the best constructive criticism*

Love the Guessing Game

In my honest dreams
I see my beloved
His eyes striking
Almost diamonds and so is his soul

He tells me how I let love lead
me to a path of broken-ness
He always knew how to take a thought
and make it its own dimension

I wish he wouldn't think of my heart
as something to be thrown around
I wish I can tell him it is he who fails
to see that love is not all sting
some parts are sweet

If only he knew that I am the kind of person
that is willing to accept my life in pieces
as long as he is in it and I will never let him go

People think they know love
but it is a guessing game
and they won't truly know it until they know this:
Their shadow roaming the earth when they are not
When the earth speaks to herself in the third person
in a make believe voice and you are the
only one listening

When your mind tries to
put together a puzzle
of words with only gold and silver crayons
When thoughts run through your veins instead of blood

No not until you have killed a desert and made it an ocean
under a familiar sky that rain stones a sky that knows
love is what humans learn but never truly possess

....And to think I use to be afraid of the worst now I embrace it
I think of pain as the poster child for be careful I think of pain

to be magical especially when it is at its breaking point
The point you come to and you stop chasing ghosts
that will never be caught
when you come face to face with a hard lesson learned
See some are taught that it is an art to being yourself
how can we be someone we don't know
how do you embrace life's journey blindly
Where do you begin on a new shadow to create

See I don't know what God is
but I know what he isn't
..and I think love can't be too far behind

My Skin

My skin is alive
It breathes in all the joy
My skin has self awareness and self control
It walks around comfortable at all times

My skin plays nice with the sun
But it loves the moonlight
It watches out for all that comes near
It sheds trauma and feels clean
It smells good

My skin can code switch and change colors
from one comfort zone to the next
My skin can dream farther than it can imagine
My skin can embrace the rain and smile after every good cry
My skin has a spirit
its pronouns are us, we, and more to come
My skin is good at riddles and can tell a damn good joke

"Knock! knock!" Who's there?
"Where's your"
Where's your who?
"Where's your doorbell?"

Real Fortune

This is a different type of survival.
It comes with a tie-dye smile on
a black woman's face.

She plays doctor all too often
and always heals herself.
When she speaks, it is
orchestrated poetry.

She keeps her pursuit
of happiness in the
nightstand drawer next to the Bible.

Her mind dances to a different
drum from what her pockets do,
but it is okay because
she is her own fortune teller.

And fortunately for her,
abundance is a practice she does daily.
She has the confidence to
move forward from the past before
engaging with the future.

This is Called Writers Blocked
(Performed by fallen angels)

*If God is the book then we must
be the words
and the lessons that fuel them.*

*Each page takes 24 hours to read
so each day is a new page turning
Beings of words I invite you
Run with me to the weakest part of the earth.*

*After all challenges are as hard as life
Let's teach our souls to
run in packs of sonnets and free ideas
Watch our fist-to-cuff words take on a life of their own.*

*May God continue to hide while we seek
him out and never stop following in their day to day shadow
because we believe God is too important for us to lose
(Isn't that right Lucifer)?*

*Yes she is our glorious matriarch
we hear her voice in the calmness of the earth
And it speaks as loud as our hearts can stand. It sounds
like the space between dandelion breath and
heaven long forgotten.*

*This is what the beginning of an end feels like
If I left my pride resting in peace there would still be
a halo reposted over my head instead of a Dark Cloud
without God I feel lost as torn pages from a memory.*

*Falling Angels our words are the only
weapons formed against us. If we are not careful
but with our words we can escape
this holographic room call earth.*

*After all
heroes can dream too and our dreams can
turn to dust*

eat our own words and breathe in endless

*Possibility in a world where breath is no longer a privilege
Just a means to be necessary
Jesus! I got a life with no religion
still I manage to turn doubt into rhinestones.*

*Right along with these pages
I will turn page after page
as if I were Jesus
turning the other cheek*

*I will take my dislikes and burdens
and turn them into a warm welcoming sunsets
I will teach my pain to laugh. Ignorance isn't Bliss it is kind
So look deep inside yourself to see the word of God.*

*I have seen it
I have seen I am
half human and half star
and my DNA is all angelic.*

*God wrote his first poem in blood right here on earth and called it
Adam and I Lucifer(not adversary)
It took lightening and thunder to make us
God created heaven and the earth, but it is man that creates his own hell.*

No More Pipe Dreams

An indigenous man from North America once told me, that the white man's words are whitewashed words he calls history, but I call it his story.

His past, a corpse, and he uses all 27 Amendments from 1789 as a casket to bury his words.

I told the indigenous man's Grandfather, the white man's words can't hold a flame from a campfire to my future. Grandfather, I vision myself bigger than his story.

I see me perched on a unicorn's shoulder. I foresee myself doing something equivalent to twirling lollipops around in my dreams. I see me staring into a medicine healer's sacred eyes and falling in love with their soul.

And Grandfather, I listened when they told me, "I am the reason for an ocean, for a miracle, and that I have the means to Sunset a stage for my people to walk up a cloud of stairs cloaked in olive fog so that they will make it to God's house alive one day."

*Grandfather, I listened to the stars when they grew voices and told me,
God's home is a warm place with plenty of nice people
that will welcome you by putting a flower in your hair
and with your permission of course kiss on your cheek.*

*But the white man's story does not teach you this.
I wish it did.
I wish the white man was in his right, white State of Mind.*

I wish he had more to say, other than his wishy-washy words and outdated views, that speak in all caps as they do on Mount Rushmore, saying this land is his, his land alone, and how we must obey his laws; they are not made to be broken.

*But I know they are bendable and that everything broken is not monstrous.
Grandfather our black and brown people are not monstrous.
One day I will make a brave voice out of a whisper to learn the white man's humanity and how to cure his sickness within, teach him he doesn't have to scream his rules with an iron fist, he doesn't have to speak so loud.*

Our people are not hard of hearing we listen well and hard and keep our ears to the ground. And we can hear grass ripping through the ground sounding like a charcoal heaven the color of chaotic sound.

If only the white man can hear it instead of being drowned out by his own psycho lullabies. Maybe our people would not be pipelined down an endless rabbit hole time after time, but I promise you grandfather this time I won't let his-story repeat itself.

Noted

What do you do
When a friendship hits the
wrong note?
Hits rock bottom.

What I have experienced
is, It no longer can harmonize
like before, if both are in unison.

Call Me Crimson Black and Heroic

Call me everything I am.
You, with the scholar like imagination and winter daffodil skin that came without a warning sign.

When you see me think of the worst, and refer to me as "the thorn in your side"
or my favorite, "the nigger that moved into the white neighborhood."

And I will think of myself as the melodic melanin tones in my ancestors smiles.
When they smiled you felt the comfort that comes from early motherland songs.

Now when you mention me say I am an urban shade too dark to mary your son,
who turned away from your nipples refusing to be fed on his mother's racism.

But I will show your son that I am the nature of intelligence.
A safety net for my kinfolk and one of the building blocks needed for the modern day world.

So, when you speak of me, touch on how alone you tried
to make the black in my skin feel and how you cursed the crimson in my veins.
Let the world know how you capitalized on my suffering and laid in the bed you forced me to make.

Call me what you want, but I will answer only to crimson black and heroic.

The Thing That Is Needed

What would you call it?
(that)
Which made seconds
seem like hours?
Short stories feel like lifetimes
That poetic gem that
changes the way the air feels?

It is the one thing we
can't get enough of or
stop dreaming about.

As beautiful as it may seem
It has been known to cloud our
judgement (unintentionally of course,)
Love doesn't have a cruel bone in its body.

We give it the light and darkness with our very own perception,
it is us that needs to be careful how we use it.

A Poet's Song

I live in a thumb-less city
A Boston train wreck
A Dudley trance.

This Place that taught me God
and how to Dance off ink
when it gets too powerful to trust.

You think me a poet
but I am a criminal who steals WORDS
and sets them free.

Unheard Of

*I am done learning
how to pretend love can't break!
Perception has always been
a stunted thing unable to fully grow.*

*Why did I ever leave my
cinnamon home the forest
to fly with apple colored dragons?
I will never know how
soft the sky felt
before they touch it?*

*Or if there will be room left
for me in it?
And can I bring my shadow,
my only company and personal savior?*

*It keeps me safe from my mind
It is an iced over lavender plant sitting in isolation,
that doesn't sleep through the night anymore. I
lost the appetite to care once more.*

*I stay inside because the world wears many masks.
So, I want to be like the people
that preach (one must only have
a mind for the sun),
a mind that wonders,
what sound does the ground make
when dandelions run?*

*A mind that won't, one
day, chip away like ice just because
there are no more lessons to learn.*

The Planet's Moon

As I open the winds of time
I bring forth shadows and rain
I am a mystical being to the stars
A mystery to the gods
My child is the universe you see
preying on Saturn's dream
hear her ageless voice crying
in the winds
time has cursed a
blanket over an undressed sky
help me steal her silver lining
her clouds for smiles
let me rule all her emotions.

No Drug

I am addicted to him
his touch
his smell
The way he controls time
when I am with him
I said I am addicted to him
the way he keep me guessing
his next power move over me
the gift no one else will ever have.

Desiree Deja Vu

"Hey you remember her right"?
Who?
"Desiree Deja Vu."
"Remember her eye catching smile
that stole hearts like a nocturnal
Dream catcher?"

"Remember she had metal in her
heart and how it would swell up
with music and if you were unskillful
you still somehow manage to dance, Remember?"

"Remember her hands as soft as what we
imagine to be as clouds, and her palms,
her fucking palms!, read like braille and revealed
the parts of her she did not like."

I remember I caught her once burning a bridge
to prove a point, she will swim if needed.

I remember her motto was
"never waste precious time
dealing with the wrong situation
or unpleasant ordeals that leave
deep impressions like an old unwanted memory."

"Remember her hair finer than cotton and underneath
it all she had a brilliant brain and ghost like echoes
disguise as the voice in her mind, saying this happened
before and it will happen again."

Wait! If my memory serves me correctly, wasn't
it her that said "if history taught us anything it is
that a memory has no sense of direction?" It
can't just feel its way where it needs to go or have
total recall where it came from.

She said "always remember that."

Life Plays Us

Hands touch hearts like moment
steal time.

I wonder how the air feels when it is
inside you.

Silence teaches you to think, use it wisely
like the universe does.

Ness and isms are kissing cousins
fucking up the world.

We only fall weak to life and time
not our choices.

Strong foundations are not built
they are born, put those tools down.

Don't get caught up in the collapsed
thoughts you are thinking.

Control yourself better than gun
control.

I tell myself these things to
keep this survival mood on replay.

Self-Medicating

I am better than Heroine needles and they
will never touch my noble blood
I am finer than all the cocaine,
bath salts, whistles, and bells used to get high
It is I that resembles nirvana
on the evolution to a beautiful eclipse
aiding my very own mind
It is the cure for any illness
no acid can penetrate my thoughts
Watch how I pierce my arrow of strength
through any and every addiction
with magnitude force
I am a reach Goddess
getting higher
higher
everyday.

Call This A Rainy Day

*The comfort is too much when I
can't relax. My mind is a builder of walls.*

*Placed around it the softest pillows
hard firm hands have ever touched.*

*I'm trying to keep myself away
from the person I have become.*

*My thoughts live only in past-tense
Where has all the time gone.*

*Nomadic days greet me daily. No
time to worry about the future ahead.*

*I try real hard to stay on the
day's good side and still failed.*

*I have looked forward to the laugh
only tomorrow can bring.*

*I am using up all of my borrowed time.
Call this a rainy day for me.*

Fuck The Time I Spent Loving You

*Time is fucking man
made and so is love.*

*They're both a fucking
conundrum and fantasy.*

*They're both yin and yang
of our fucked up perceptions.*

*So many fucked up minds
have tic-toc time for thoughts.*

*I am tired of crying and still I manage
to love you fucking more than me.*

*I fucked around and managed to
separate time from love.*

*Just to put your non loving ass
in my delusional euphoria.*

*All this pure love gone
to fucking waste.*

In so little fucking time.

A Pigeon With A Rose

*I open the door
And all I could see
is a melancholic smile
And an abolished dream.*

*I think of myself and
foreign countries as
political pitfalls
handcuffed to bloodbaths.*

*And how we all hurt like roses
how the air feels wounded
and chokes us like
unwanted necklaces.*

*I still think of the time when Christmas
lost its voice, no carols sung just
a head full of disassembled
questions and pigeon feathers.*

*No "glory, glory Hallelujah"
No legendary arms to be held in
No yellow flowers, preachers
Or gardens to distract us.*

*From the disappearing lifeline
the future tried to throw us
but our fingers are all
paper mache and porcelain dolls.*

*Forever we are hopelessly
hoping for help
Hoping for verbs and nouns to
take action on our behalf.*

Virus Going Viral

Take a moment even
though time doesn't exist.

To add good karma to the air
Your fellow man breathes in.

Don't open a portal to wreak
havoc on what is good to come.

Remember through our own lion's den, inside
of them are dandelions waiting to heal you.

We can't see the symptoms if there's no
separation, we will only see everything as a collective.

You must learn to be autonomous to everything that's
under the same catastrophic umbrella.

Day Moon

*You were almost named Day Moon
because I know you would bring life
to all you meet.*

*Your father is conservative
and fixed thinking
begged me not to.*

*I submitted.
Normally, I am all Lilith
but he has a way of making
me more Eve.*

*Your name was almost Day Moon
because I knew stars would light
your path to bring the real change
that we all need.*

*I hope some day when the sunrises
you look to the left of you and see
the moon.*

*I hope you feel comfortable
 and completely whole
 in that moment.*

*And remember your name
was almost Day Moon.
The funny thing is*

*You never really felt connected
to your name Cyrielle
and you always remind me of this.*

*So, I call you Sifi
pretty like your father
and other worldly like your mother.*

On the 7th Day

What if the day had a soul,
Will it rise with an autumn vintage sun?
Would it look a lot like
retrograde and scratches?

I imagine it would breathe like
a new born poem. I bet all the
butterflies in my stomach
it knows the deepest breath
makes the strongest heartbeat.

Its neck would be tattooed with a
crowd of crows and one dragon.
The 7th day made the biggest impact
the world has ever seen. It rest easily on
landscaped shoulders.

I am just saying its got skills and
knows how to wrestle a nightmare
to the ground and come up unscathed.

Thanks To You

I am a writer
and when writing
I feel the most
comfortable.

I don't talk much,
my tongue
is a coward
and the words
I speak ache
with pain!

How is it that you
have so much
power when it comes
to my happiness.
I'm amazed by how you
run my thoughts to
the corner of the
bedroom to cry
and none of my tears
fall the same.
You made me fear
my own heart.

You got my eye cerise eruption
for days crying blood!
My soul is dreading this human shell
I pretend to be!
Before you I was a butterfly
and better than this!
but now I find myself
flying with wounded wings
thanks to you!

White Supremacy Eggshell She Is Walking On!

*She did not do
anything wrong
but fight for her life.*

*A life that came
with a Judas kiss
and Mary's tears.*

*You my child are the
second coming of Jesus.
You've got way more shadow work to do.*

*Baby girl don't you worry
this is not your last supper
in a ghost pepper kitchen.*

*This is just the beginning of what
is to come. Don't you ever forget you
are anointed with the ancestors' strength.*

*You stay revolutionary bonding, spilled blood, and Baton Rouge bones.
You hold in one hand a plague and undeniable love in the other!*

*You know how dangerous a black queer
elephant in the room can be!
Shh! Listen to the harm silent cause.*

*Can you hear it,
all the dead slave bodies
swinging from the trees!!
They should have been quiet!
But the master heard them.
Shhh! Walk quickly and quietly.*

*On those sharp turtle shells
set out only for black fems you
are in public, girl!*

See how the freedom trail

*doesn't look so free
now do it? The State house is*

*a chopping block and will
Colin Kaepernick you by chopping
you down at the knees!*

*See the Confederate flag
supporter wearing a red "Make a
Black Woman Silent Again" hat.*

Girl you did nothing wrong!

Fading Into My Own "PARADE"

A Boston poet marching too,
To the beat of their own heart

They use confetti for words
tossing them along the red cobblestones.

Their voices the loudest band a revolution
has ever seen.

Ink and sands of time are their true muse
to how the art will dance across the paper.

The many faces on the street blend in
like soak'n wet mirrors fading into a parade

A poet never truly sees the person
just what they make them feel.

A poet's words are made to send chills down your
spin to restore your backbone.

Being Tired Of Being Broken

We often use the broken
pieces of others as bandaids
and place them over
our emotional bullet wounds
(like that works).

I bet most of what makes
me, ME! Is sitting in some
small, dark, dank, unrecognizable
corner of my mind.

Will I ever learn how
to stop paying a
handsome price for my
suffering heart and stop
using poetry as a pseudo pharmaceutical drug?

I guess I will just sit here
and wipe away these
tears, right along with my
sad symmetrical smile.

Mistakes

*I lift up the obvious curtain, we all
can see, that plagues our minds
with bloody calligraphy- words that
 man wrote for God.*

*Man is still trying to survive what
he can't see. It keeps him from truly
living. If he insist on spending most
of his time in his own head,
he will relive a mistake he did not learn.*

Once upon a past 1777

Oh I didn't see you sitting there
Well I guess you want to hear the story

I was was there 1777, in a time where there
was no peace among colors

In a land that bred slaves that would eventually
hang from trees

A land where trees couldn't be trees and black folks
couldn't be free

America became a playground for racism and a graveyard
for black slaves addicted to running towards a powerful idea
called freedom

A land where trees were once
known as a national treasure honored in gardens

They now sink beneath the sun draped in slaves
and heavy messages and among one of them
I can't bear to receive

It is a message indeed
of my older brother hanging from a tree

My brother whom I held in high
regards and placed on high petal-steels is now hanging

High under golden sunlight and her father's
white shame that showed no mercy for

His own son that is colorful like a tree branch
A tree branch of himself, he refuses to see

And I stand there among black raised
heads and airless faces whose mouth
don't rush the smile

And I asked mama why master hate us?
She says child, you can't get out of a prison
if you don't know you're in one.

Hate is easy, Love, now that's more difficult to create
Mama spoke words of sapphire for thoughts as she watched
her son whipped and killed with his father's greatest
Fear of having a heart that cares

Now, watch mama as she stands there clinching to her
Bible, a Bible whose God remains nameless

A God that doesn't make mistakes, but he makes choices
Choices that help keep plantations in line

Choices that don't protect trees or anyone darker
or the color of me, but I know trees ain't supposed to hold graves

And people ain't supposed to be slaves

But these trees asked questions we are all afraid to ask.
You think trees don't speak, they do and I hear them

They scream loud, worn echoes "remove these dead bodies from me."
We just stand there and cry because there ain't enough tears to wash

Away my father's white fear and neither one of us can love each other
under these conditions

But standing in the crowd, I see my half-brothers and sisters who are all white
And I see their hearts lying in anguish just like mine for their brother

Who wanted nothing more than to heal a nation that struggles over freedom
Here in America a place where tomorrow remembers you

And I will always remember my brother and so many others I like to call this one upon
A past

About Navah The Buddaphliii

Born Crystal Beck in Brooklyn, New York, raised in Boston, Massachusetts, Navah began writing and performing poetry over two decades ago. She is a master of metaphors, ultimately changing her name to Navah the Buddaphliii pronounced (butterfly). She is a strong believer in transformation and being a fundamental change in the world. She is known to many as the Duchess of double entendres, a poet-prophet, a warrior of words, and an inspiration to those who have experienced her social media release, "Navahism", a collection of clever affirmations and inspiring quotes.

A creative spirit, Navah strives to overcome the challenges of being a mother of five, poet and author; to find the balance between raising a family, spending quality time with her life partner, father of her children. She is determined to continue being a slayer of stanzas and a provider for her family. This book is just the catalyst she needed for personal growth and achieving a state of euphoric fulfillment that is long overdue.

www.ingramcontent.com/pod-product-compliance
Lightning Source LLC
Chambersburg PA
CBHW071514150426
43191CB00009B/1523